Samuel Beckett's *Krapp's Last Tape*

D1474747

"We lay there without moving. But under us all moved, and moved us."

– Krapp

Samuel Beckett's most accessible play is also one of the twentieth century's most moving dramas about aging, memory, and disappointment. Daniel Sack offers the first comprehensive survey of *Krapp's Last Tape* (1958) with a general reader in mind.

Structured around a series of questions, five approachable sections contextualize the play in the larger career of its Nobel-Prize-winning writer explore its major thematic concerns, and offer comparative analyses with Beckett's other signal works. Sack also uses discussions of significant productions, including those directed by the playwright himself, to ground interpretation of the play in terms of its performance and provide a useful resource to directors and actors.

Both a critical and personal exploration of this haunting play, this volume is a must-read for anyone with an interest in Beckett's work.

Daniel Sack is Assistant Professor in the English Department and Commonwealth Honors College at the University of Massachusetts Amherst.

The Fourth Wall

The Fourth Wall series is a growing collection of short books on famous plays. Its compact format perfectly suits the kind of fresh, engaging criticism that brings a play to life.

Each book in this series selects one play or musical as its subject and approaches it from an original angle, seeking to shed light on an old favourite or break new ground on a modern classic. These lively, digestible books are a must for anyone looking for new ideas on the major works of modern theater.

Also available in this series:

Coming soon:

Samuel Beckett's *Krapp's Last Tape*

Daniel Sack

Routledge
Taylor & Francis Group

LONDON AND NEW YORK

First published 2016
by Routledge
2 Park Square, Milton Park, Abingdon, Oxon OX14 4RN

and by Routledge
711 Third Avenue, New York, NY 10017

Routledge is an imprint of the Taylor & Francis Group, an informa business

© 2016 Daniel Sack

British Library Cataloguing-in-Publication Data
A catalogue record for this book is available from
the British Library

Library of Congress Cataloguing-in-Publication Data
A catalog record for this title has been requested

ISBN: 9781138961265 (pbk)
ISBN: 9781315659879 (ebk)

Typeset in Bembo
by Out of House Publishing

Contents

Acknowledgments

Thanks to Joe Kelleher for beginning this journey. To the students in my undergraduate seminar "Beckett across the Arts" for conversation along the way. To John McBratney for eyes (and a camera) on the ground in Dublin. To Jane Degenhardt for her friendship and insight. To Elisabeth Barnick for careful reading. And, finally, to Ben Piggott for sharing my excitement about this most beautiful and haunting of plays.

Note: all in-text references to *Krapp's Last Tape* refer to the Grove Press edition of *The Selected Works of Samuel Beckett*, Vol. III: *Dramatic Works* (New York, 2010).

1

What happens

> *Be again, be again.* (Pause.) *All that old misery.* (Pause.) *Once wasn't enough for you.*
>
> *Krapp's Last Tape*

In the end of 1957 – four years after the premiere of *Waiting for Godot* (*En attendant Godot* in the original French) brought sudden international recognition to a writer who had toiled for close to three decades in relative obscurity – Samuel Beckett heard selections from his prose pieces *Molloy* and *From an Abandoned Work* read by the Irish actor Patrick Magee on BBC radio. Or, rather, Beckett couldn't quite hear the broadcast clearly from his home in Paris, so he visited the Parisian office of the BBC and listened to the recording on a reel-to-reel player there (Knowlson 1996, 444).

The Irish author had been living in self-imposed exile in France for more than twenty-five years and had written the bulk of his greatest texts from the late 1940s onwards in his second language – French – only translating the texts back into English after the fact. He had composed in a foreign tongue to alienate his language, to dislocate himself from the conventions and influences that had marred his earlier attempts at original expression. Hearing Magee speak these words in the cadences of his abandoned homeland apparently left a deep impression on Beckett. Immediately afterwards, he began the play – originally titled *Magee Monologue* – that would become *Krapp's Last Tape* a short six drafts and three weeks later. After composing his work in French for more than a decade, it was the first play he would write directly in English. And so, from the start, the play circled around a disembodied voice from a distant time and place, locked in a loop of memory passing from reel to reel.

Krapp's Last Tape is Beckett's most personal and most autobiographical creation. It is, perhaps, his most accessible work, his most realistic, and, perhaps too, his most moving. Beckett's dramatic universe features worlds in which couples are consigned to trash bins (*Endgame*) or reduced to purgatorial imprisonment in urns (*Play*), worlds where a woman can be buried in a mound of earth up to her waist or neck (*Happy Days*), or reduced to a mere mouth speaking endlessly in the dark (*Not I*). These images of capture and claustrophobia sear themselves into one's memory the way a recurring nightmare might resound interminably unresolved. Against these, *Krapp's Last Tape* is the closest thing to everyday reality that Beckett would write for the stage. Indeed, we might recognize Krapp sitting night after night in the darkened corner of our local pub, bar, or café. The bartender might whisper about that man enclosed alone in drink – the failed author, the failed lover. We might see our future selves reflected in his stare, looking back.

So it was with me, when I first read the play in my freshman year of university, some fifteen years ago. I saw Krapp as a future I might inherit. At the time I thought myself an actor and a writer. I knew I was too young to play Krapp, but I feared I was already preparing for the role. For what if a script were a forecast, a kind of promise about how your life might unfold? Isn't this what all dramatic scripts offer us – the outline of a prospective event to inhabit some day? The published script of the play begins with the suggestive time signature, *A late evening in the future*. Frightening words. Premonitions of a time at the other end of this time, not just an evening in the future, but on the far side of that future evening, too late to be up and yet sleepless, pacing or poring over material in half-light. We could certainly make the case that Beckett saw his future self in the faded writer, that the *late evening in the future* would be his own time many years hence: a portrait of the artist as an old man. So one wonders *who* happens in this play – the character, the author, or the audience/reader? The timeless voice or the aging body?

We will return to these questions in the next section of this book, but before exploring the identity of Krapp, it makes sense to ask *what* happens to him, and to thus provide a brief outline of the play.

At the curtain's rise we see an old man – Krapp – sitting there at a small table lit amid the dark. He faces out, looking over a reel-to-reel tape recorder with microphone and, beside it, a pile of boxes. Checking his watch with a "great sigh," as if to see if it is really time for the performance, he begins his ritual. Each year, near midnight of his birthday, he plays out the same game: he records his musings on the year past, using the tape recorder as a kind of audio diary. But first, he listens to a recording from an earlier year – perhaps to get himself in the mood, perhaps to mark the passage of time even more clearly.

The man is something of an old clown. Dressed in ridicu-lous clothes, white-faced with a "purple nose" and an awkward walk, he eats a banana or two and slips on the peel. His name may have fated him to a certain scatological orientation, which does not escape his bitter amusement and regret. Intermittently over the next half-hour he will stumble into a back room and pop open a bottle, succumbing to the vice of steady drink he has struggled to avoid for years. After his slapstick maneuvers, he begins in earnest, pulling out one of the reels in the boxes on his table. Relishing some over the sounds in his mouth – "Spool! (*pause.*) Spooool!" (218) – he reads out from a ledger the contents of the tape he has unearthed: "Mother at rest at last [. . .] The black ball [. . .] The dark nurse [. . .] memorable equinox [. . .] Farewell to . . . love" (219). He loads the tape into the machine and presses "play."

A younger voice announces itself and we watch as Krapp listens to a recording from thirty years past. His 39-year-old self describes how he has, in turn, just finished listening to a tape from ten or twelve years back when Krapp was in his late twenties (27 or 29). This middle Krapp soon launches into his own "postmortem" on his thirty-ninth year. At first, the oldest Krapp identifies with the middle Krapp's mock-ery of the still-younger Krapp in short laughs, but he soon begins to stray from that identification. Old Krapp mocks his younger self for his false preening, and yet presents himself a paler version of the same man. He cannot remember the meaning of words that readily sprang to mind in his prime, and is forced to look up the peculiar "viduity" in an old dic-tionary. Gone, too, is the memory of the ball he was throw-ing to a small dog outside the hospital when his mother passed away, though his younger voice is certain that "I shall feel it, in my hand, until my dying day" (222). The material experience of memory is no more; all that remains is the description of a recollection.

When the account of the "memorable equinox" comes on, Krapp revolts visibly. He manually fast-forwards the tape, desperate to skip over the event. We can piece together only so much: a night alone at the water's edge, great winds tossing the waves. Krapp recounts that in this moment it became:

> clear to me at last that the dark I have always struggled to keep under is in reality – (*Krapp curses, switches off, winds tape forward, switches on again*) – unshatterable association until my dissolution of storm and night with the light of the understanding and the fire—.
>
> (222)

It sounds a textbook experience of the romantic sublime, where an individual confronts a worldly expanse that dwarfs all capacity to know or say and leaves one stupid, speechless. It seems that the darkness, ignorance, and failure that Krapp had kept at bay are here recognized as his source of strength. But listening from the other side of time, the older Krapp knows that the epiphany and the purported devotion to his work it will inspire lead nowhere.

Krapp skips ahead and suddenly he is in the midst of another sublime encounter. In lyrical language he describes an afternoon spent on a punt (rowboat) with a woman, during which Krapp decided to end their relationship. He lingers on the memory of her dark eyes staring up as "[w]e lay there without moving. But under us all moved, and moved us, gently, up and down, and from side to side" (223). If the scene on the pier presented the unfathomable depths of the world, here the sublime belongs to another person – to a lover abandoned. In both cases, the encounter exposes the intensely private Krapp to the movement of a world beyond his control.

At the end of this intimate reminiscence, the oldest Krapp stops, drinks, and loads a new reel onto the machine to record his account of the past year.

It sounds a painfully diminished life: his great *magnum opus* forgotten, his outings reduced to occasional couplings with a "bony old ghost of a whore" (224), and a visit to a church, where he nods off in the pews. He wants nothing more than to lie back in the dark and "wander" in his memories: to "[b]e again in the dingle on a Christmas Eve, gathering holly, the red-berried. (*Pause.*) Be again on Croghan on a Sunday morning, in the haze, with the bitch, stop and listen to the bells" (225). These are Irish places: the dingle a peninsula off the southwest, and Croghan (Crohan) a mountain in county Wicklow, just south of Dublin. Places where Beckett himself spent his youth. It is sensation that grounds these memories, not story or language, and his reverie returns at its end to the image of the woman on the punt, lingering again on her eyes.

For Krapp, the past holds far more interest and desire than the present: he stops the machine and wrenches the tape free, in order to reload the earlier recording. He winds it to the passage about the punt again, listening intently and trying to recapture that fleeting moment. His younger self concludes: "Perhaps my best years are gone. When there was a chance of happiness. But I wouldn't want them back. Not with the fire in me now. No, I wouldn't want them back" (226). It is clear to us that these words could not be more false, though it is less certain whether Krapp himself can see his tragic misapprehension. He stares out into the surrounding darkness, while the tape runs on in silence to its end.

It is a short play: some ten pages in *The Selected Works of Samuel Beckett* and usually some thirty to forty minutes in performance. And yet, as with Beckett's other increasingly brief late works for the stage, a great deal coils around this small, contained event. Three different ages of Krapp appear onstage – a whole lifetime represented in this short span of time. And the questions raised are hugely existential, even universal. Can a person change or do the lies we repeatedly tell ourselves reveal our most certain character? How does personal desire intersect with ambition, the sensual with the intellectual? What does it mean to listen to oneself at a remove, to see oneself as another? These thematic concerns are integrated into the very structure of the play; they are *how* the play makes its meanings, as we will see in the third section of this book. Inevitably, in a play so concerned with time, this folds over into the following section's questions of *when* time plays out. What is memory? Can it be controlled – cut off, or rewound and replayed? Or does remembered sensation only arise unbidden? Is life lived or remembered?

I have been describing the play as outlined in the stage directions of the first published edition (printed in the *Evergreen Review* in the summer of 1958, then in 1959 by Faber in the UK, and in 1960 by Grove Press in the USA). But Beckett returned to the play repeatedly over the next decades of his life, consulting on productions and eventually directing several of his own. In fact, it may be the play that Beckett revisited most often in his career. We will have a chance to explore the subtle refinements he made to the piece in the pages that follow. But we will also spend some while looking at significant productions by other directors. These often hinge on the performance of the actor playing Krapp, a role that has attracted some of the greatest performers of the last fifty years, including Brian Dennehy, Michael Gambon, John Hurt, Harold Pinter, and Robert Wilson, to name but a few who have played Krapp in English since the turn of the millennium (in the interest of brevity, this book only glances at the equally extensive performance history of the play in French or German). We will also consider some of the fundamental difficulties and fascinations with the text in performance. While I gesture occasionally to individual inter-pretations throughout the sections that follow, the fifth and final section focuses on *where* the play happens by looking at the specific choices made in particular productions by actors, designers, and directors, including Beckett himself.

A last thought before I get under way in earnest. Linger for a moment longer on this word "last." Krapp's last tape might be his final one, suggesting that he has given up on the ritual of recording or that this is his final year on earth. Death waits in the wings or just upstage. Indeed, when Beckett directed the play, he had Krapp glance behind him into the darkness several times, unconsciously checking in case some spirit of the end drew close. When directing the piece, he confided to an actor playing the part that "the man [Krapp] is dead the next day" (Kalb 1989, 212). "Last" also might refer to his previous tape which becomes the centerpiece of his current rumination. In this previous tape, his prior self reflects on a still earlier tape: the *last* last tape. In other words, each present tape responds to the one before. Or it might refer to the fact that the tape he records now is his most recent, that he will repeat this game of remembrance next year. Finally, we might also consider the fact that these tapes themselves last; looping ghosts that retain their grasp, they haunt him and us, lastingly. All these meanings are true at once and they collect Beckett's nuanced apprehension of time in a single four-letter curse: last.

2

Who happens

It's been a long time now since I first read *Krapp's Last Tape*, many years since I sat in my dorm room, whispering the text into a cassette recorder, relishing the sound of my own voice saying "spoool" alongside Krapp. It felt appropriate to read these words aloud so that I might then hear myself speaking them again, at some distance. At once a kind of ward to prevent myself from living Krapp's path of lonesome regret and an invocation to call the figure into existence, I would play the words back again and again, walking across campus or sitting backstage during a rehearsal with my headphones attached to a neon yellow Sony Walkman. I was an actor back then and I was practising for the day when I would be able to take up this part, to my mind one of the greatest in the English language.

When I started writing this book, I sought out the cassette in my childhood home, sifting through dusty shoeboxes filled with mixtapes and my first albums – Paul Simon's *Graceland*, Cat Stevens's *Greatest Hits*. While it was not quite Krapp's expanse of thirty years between speaking and listening, still I wondered how I would sound these fifteen years removed.

Would I be able hear any difference in the amber of a cassette tape? Am I the same person that I was yesterday, let alone fifteen or thirty years ago?

Krapp's Last Tape is a portrait play that asks us to reflect upon the nature of character and its consistencies across time. Who is Krapp? The stage directions tell us little, leaning heavily on a rather peculiar word and saying simply that he is "a wearish old man" (217). "Wearish," the *Oxford English Dictionary* tells us, means obsolete, or "void of relish, insipid, savourless; flat, futile, ineffectual." In a wonderfully cyclical manner, the word itself is no longer in use – it is an obsolete way of describing the obsolete. Here is a figure who has lost all savour for the world, for whom language itself has become somewhat hollowed, and who – despite his occasional trysts with the "bony old whore" Fanny and his weepy longing for the protagonist of Theodor Fontane's novel *Effi Briest* (1894) – feels himself impotent both romantically and creatively. Everything that was once full of life and variation has been sucked dry and he appears before us as the husk of a man. (In another loop of language I will discuss below, the name "Krapp" too recalls an obsolete word for the husks removed from grain.)

His world is gathering close about him: his hearing and eyesight are leaving him so that he has to squint to read, has to lean in close to hear the words his more forceful, younger self speaks. No passive consumer, he has to work at listening. The only prop of note, a heavy silver pocketwatch and chain, literalizes the fact that he is also anchored by the weight of time. The clothing he wears – ill-fitting, "rusty," and "grimy" – as well as his unshaven visage and disordered hair, bespeak a carelessness with regards to his appearance. Yet the waistcoat, white shirt, "surprising pair of dirty white boots" (217), and that silver pocketwatch together indicate he was once a man of some means, perhaps even a dandy of sorts. There is no mention of a job, so he may come from independent fortune, enough to have devoted his attentions to the composition of his life's work, a book that has been a great disappointment.

Beckett's first, failed attempted at playwriting obliquely foretells Krapp's situation and might give us a glimpse at some version of the character's earlier self. Unproduced and unpublished during the playwright's lifetime, *Eleuthéria* (1947) centers on the family Krap (one 'p' less) and follows the son, Victor, as he opts out of domestic and social action. Like his older future descendant Krapp, he abandons love, and absents himself from attending the death of a parent – in this case, his father instead of his mother. Victor Krap is not a writer; he does not have any role to play and would rather stay in bed, doing nothing as a way of claiming his own potentiality freed from social obligations. He excuses himself from justifying a lack of action: "One aspect of his freedom," as Hugh Kenner writes, is a "freedom from the necessity to devise explanations, even for his own enlightenment" (Kenner 1961, 141). The later Krapp does little else besides explain his past – either a distant past in the 39-year-old's recording or the more immediate one in the 69-year-old's – though that explanation does not lead to any greater enlightenment.

What else does he do with himself? His purple nose and frequent trips to the back room to uncork a bottle signal that Krapp still indulges in the alcohol that he resolved to cut out thirty years before. So, too, does he eat his bananas with a mindless automatism; he will devour his first banana rapidly and blindly, then suddenly come to himself and notice with disgust that he has consumed nearly all of a second banana without even being aware of what he has done. There is something mechanical about this habit-driven living.

The middle-aged Krapp wields obscure words like "viduity" with smug ease, advertising his sophistication and speaking with a polished eloquence. If the older Krapp relishes anything, it is not the words as carriers of meaning but sound itself. What used to be a pleasure in the play of language has been reduced to an appreciation of speech's materiality, its mouthfeel. He discovers the "happiest moment of the past half million" (224) in his elongated ululation, "spoool", as if to evidence old age as a second infancy. He caresses sound, tests its weight, even sings now, where once his younger self found the possibility of song inconceivable. The French actor Pierre Chabert, who performed the part on several occasions, perceptively suggests "Krapp plays with the word as if it were a fetish or a talisman. He literally feels it; he explores it musically and gesturally" (Chabert in Knowlson 1980, 94). Losing the language, Krapp moves towards becoming pure voice.

That is the Krapp we see before us, but there are two other Krapps nested in the play who have, indeed, become only voice: the 39-year-old we hear on the tape, and, as recounted by this middle-aged character, the younger one still. We might presume that the younger one has, in turn, listened to someone even younger and so on, like a set of Russian dolls receding back until that smallest inarticulate memory of infancy. These other Krapps coil around the unheard spools that fill the unopened boxes piled atop the desk; one scholar's calculation suggests there are forty-five recordings on the stage, a host of silent Krapps surrounding him (Knowlson 1992, 19). Each of us holds within him- or herself numberless prior selves, but here we are faced with the peculiar experience of encountering these various players at once, in conversation as it were, with others waiting in the wings.

And so, even if he remains a lone figure, isolated onstage and in life, repeating the refrain "not a soul" (219, 224) as if surveying a wasteland he alone occupied, the Krapp we see onstage is divided. This one performer plays both speaker and listener to his own speech. It is a proposition that Beckett would explore again later in his short play *Ohio Impromptu* (1980). There, two identical figures sit at the same table, mirrored in poses of intense attention with a hand resting on the brow and obscuring the face, one listening to the other read from a book for the duration. It is unclear who wrote that volume, but the words read draw asymptotically closer to describing the scene of the performance itself – without ever arriving at actual identification. Perhaps these two are the same person riven by the great loss at which the read story hints – a partner dead or gone – perhaps one is a projection of the other; we do not know. Listening to ourselves recorded or reading what we once wrote, we become another. Any story told becomes something other than lived experience.

If *Ohio Impromptu* literalizes this divide by splitting the speaker from the listener, then in *Krapp's Last Tape* those two different roles are seemingly carried in the same body. The stage directions describe a "cracked voice" with "distinctive intonation" for the elder Krapp and a "strong voice, rather pompous" for the recorded, middle-aged version. This presents a challenge for the actor: he must record and perform live two different versions of himself, and this difference in age must be apparent from voice alone. He must scrub clean the intangible detritus of his own time and pretend a youthful diffidence or add age's imagined texture to his clarion proclamations. In either case, underneath whatever quality is added, we must recognize that this is the same person speaking, that it bears the same "grain of the voice," as the French critic

Roland Barthes names it (Barthes 1977) – the edges of flesh and contours of resonance that distinguish the peculiar character of one's voice from any other. "For surely," as Chabert puts it, "one of the most disturbing aspects of the acting should lie in this relationship between two voices, different yet similar; a voice that is a strange echo of itself" (Knowlson 1980, 90). It would be entirely wrong to cast another performer to read these lines.

In the shoebox again, I find cassettes with handwritten titles long since faded away, or a single date in a hand at once like and unlike my own (my father's? my mother's?). I put these in the player and hear the squeak of childhood come up, a round sung with occasional laughs cutting in – "this is the song that never ends," "ninety-nine bottles of beer on the wall." I am not alone in feeling an uncanny discomfort whenever I hear a recording of my voice, even if that speech arrives from the most recent past. Stranger still to listen to the child I once was, some contour of my present cadence in that high, lisping voice. But strangest of all to hear myself when I was an "adult," yet time had not marked its peculiar signature on the surface of my sound. I seem the same person and yet not the same. So it was when I heard myself playing Krapp again. It sounded like I was already onstage, that my voice was playing a character that resembled myself but in a costume that fit loose in places, needed to be drawn in. I laughed at the serious tone taken by that young man who discussed love and loss as if he knew their texture. And when he laughed in mockery because the script told him to do so, I laughed too, without knowing whether I laughed at him or alongside him. There are things in this story too close to home, too maudlin for the page. Suffice to say I know Krapp better now than I did then.

I'm not alone in seeing myself in both versions of Krapp and finding discomfort facing the reflection. Ruby Cohn, one of the first and greatest of Beckett's critics, wrote towards the end of her life about her own knotted relationship to a play she never really liked. "As my senses dim, but I retain enough memory to realize how faulty it is, I see bits of Beckett in *Krapp's Last Tape* and much of myself. It doesn't make me like the play any better" (Cohn 2006, 523). I can't tell whether Cohn is saying that her discomfort with the play derives from a discomfort with herself. It certainly has made the writing of this small book a surprisingly unsettling process for me as I discover versions of myself in the descriptions of Krapp I keep revising.

Who can say where volition sits in this relationship? Do we choose to write about ourselves or does the writing find us out unawares? Where Beckett generally refused to acknowledge any biographical connection to his writing, it was clear to those performers who worked with him that, of all his creations, Krapp cleaved most closely to the writer himself. Martin Held, the German actor in the first production of the play that Beckett directed at the Schiller Theater in 1969, decided to incorporate the hand deformations from which the Irish writer suffered in his later life into his portrayal of the part. (Beckett had what is called Dupuytren's contracture, a condition that prevents the extension of one or two fingers and fixes the hand in a claw-like grasp at all times.) As the two were working on the part, Held slowly began to take on this physical gesture, an acting choice he made of his own accord: "[Beckett] looked at it once and just said, 'Good,'" Held explains; "there is an amazing amount of Beckett in Krapp" (Knowlson 1980, 186). Beckett would confide as much to the actor Jean Martin when he directed him in a

French production of the play: "[Beckett] told me very precisely about the genesis of the play, the personal links between himself and Krapp" (Knowlson 1980, 81).

Let us attend to these "bits of Beckett" that Cohn and others have seen in Krapp. Samuel Beckett was born in Foxrock, a suburb of Dublin, in 1906. He would study Romance languages at Trinity College Dublin, focusing on the Italian fourteenth-century poet Dante and his *Divine Comedy* trilogy about a pilgrim's passage through Inferno, Purgatory, and finally Paradise. The fictional and autobiographical walk hand in hand throughout: Dante cast himself as the protagonist, his journey towards salvation inspired by an imagined journey towards the woman he had loved and lost, Beatrice; and the people he met along his path were both mythic and actual figures from his life, suffering the consequences of their lived transgressions. In this the trilogy marks what is arguably the first written quest for depth of self-understanding. The tales of individuals trapped in the torment of their past while perpetually awaiting salvation from an inscrutable divinity would influence Beckett's writings for the remainder of his life. We might also suppose that Dante's confrontations with his past in fictional form obliquely presage Beckett's writing of Krapp as a means of reviewing his own history.

Beckett left Ireland for continental Europe soon after graduation to teach English at the Sorbonne in Paris and to expose himself to the city's vibrant artistic scene. There he met the second great influence on his writing: the novelist James Joyce, a fellow Dubliner in self-elected exile. He worked as an assistant for Joyce, whose eyesight had begun to fail him, transcribing sections of the impossibly dense text that would become *Finnegan's Wake* (1939). Still an academic of sorts, Beckett published some critical analyses of Joyce at the novelist's encouragement, and what poetry and prose he wrote in the surrounding years were heavily steeped in the elder's erudite expansiveness. Beckett wore this cultivated difficulty awkwardly, and his work from this period is at times unreadable in its pretensions. Like Krapp, Beckett knew the misery of the unread writer: he wrote two novels, a collection of short stories, and many poems over the course of the 1930s and 1940s, but was almost completely ignored. It was only in the later 1940s that Beckett realized a departure from Joyce's example.

The shift stemmed from a revelation that in many ways echoes the passage Krapp is so eager to skip in the tape from his late thirties. Beckett confided to his biographer James Knowlson that the play's epiphany on the jetty did in fact happen to him in Ireland, though not on a jetty: "Krapp's vision was on the pier at Dún Laoghaire; mine was in my mother's room" (Knowlson 1996, 319). This was sometime in 1945–1946, during one of his yearly visits to his widowed mother, when Beckett was 39 years old – the same age as Krapp when he experienced his great seaside epiphany. In conversation with Knowlson, Beckett filled in the gaps where Krapp had cut off the tape, saying that the dark was "'in reality . . . [here Krapp skips ahead, where Beckett continues] my most precious ally etc. meaning his [my] true element at last and key to the magnum opus.' Light was therefore rejected in favor of darkness" (Knowlson 1996, 319). After his own revelation, Beckett would no longer write the Joycean texts that accumulated references and quotations as if to know the world's vast array and thereby control it. Instead, he would move in the diametrically opposed direction, focusing on his interior life, the irrational, and the unknowable.

In an interview soon after the success of *Waiting for Godot*, Beckett reflected on the relationship between his work and that of Joyce: "the more Joyce knew the more he could. He's tending towards omniscience and omnipotence as an artist. I'm working with impotence, ignorance. I don't think impotence has been exploited in the past" (Shenker 1956). We might think of Krapp's impotence, his self-enclosed or constipated life, and his general ignorance about himself and his habits. In practice, this lead Beckett to progressively reduce the written, the visible, the audible – a paring-down of language to its bare bones, delimiting setting to the most immediate difference between interior and exterior life, and action to the rudiments of movement; Beckett's characters struggle to understand how to ride a bicycle; how to walk, crawl, or even roll over. *Waiting for Godot*'s wasted landscape with its tree and rock, its road between unnamed places, and its pairs of colorful characters (Vladimir and Estragon, Lucky and Pozzo, and the two boys) seems positively crowded with life and variation in comparison with the stark, barren later plays. These narrowed their worlds to a small patch of dimming light or a featureless chamber, where stunted and stilled characters are limited to meager tasks – to speak or to listen, often endlessly and without hope of alteration. The plays and texts became shorter and shorter, too, without ever becoming fragments or sketches; they are complete in themselves. The shortest of these, *Breath*, lasts a mere thirty seconds dictated by the intake and release of a single breath and seems to contain in that duration an entire lifetime, an entire world. After his epiphany, Beckett sought out the point at which a play or story might be reduced to its most minimal form.

One of the signal features of Beckett's minimalist aesthetic henceforth is its seeming dislocation from time and place. The plays and prose works often place their characters in abstract environments that blur the boundaries between the real and imagined, the living and the dead, the earthly and the otherworldly. Yet fragmentary references to Ireland and his childhood in Dublin glimmer in the otherwise uniform texture of Beckett's scoured language.

Krapp's Last Tape is striking in these regards. While the stage directions describe a small circle of light in a placeless surround, the offstage world described by Krapp is full of textured particularity, even if he cannot see it through the literal and psychological dark. The play fosters a consistent world that in no way departs from realism. And that world is arguably a version of Beckett's past, an Irish past. As Cohn puts it, "[a]lthough Krapp's den lacks an address, the overtones are Irish" (Cohn 1980, 24). It may be silent tonight, but the tones of Miss McGlome's songs from her childhood in Connaught (a western region of Ireland) usually drift in at this hour. And the memories to which Krapp returns when lying propped up in his bedbound reveries are all Irish places where Beckett himself spent his youth. This cascade of reminiscence culminates in his repetition of the refrain "lie down across her" (225), a quotation from the episode with the girl on the punt. It enforces a correlation between lost love and lost home or youth, both places of repose to which he longs to return. In this, John Fletcher and John Spurling propose that the play belongs beside two neighboring works – the prose piece *From an Abandoned Work* (1955) and the radio play *Embers* (1959) – which share "a mood of nostalgia, and atmosphere of the pastoral and idyllic, an unashamedly poetic idiom [. . .] to form a kind of triptych on the theme of lost love in an Irish landscape" (Fletcher and Spurling 1972, 89).

The influence of Irish drama is felt strongly in the plays that Beckett began to write following his epiphany in the mid-1940s and *Krapp's Last Tape* is no exception. The writer's occasional visits to the theatres of Dublin during his studies at Trinity impacted his playwriting in lasting ways, particularly the purgatorial parables of W. B. Yeats (*At the Hawks Well* from 1916, as well as his other plays inspired by the Japanese Noh Theater) and J. M. Synge (*The Well of the Saints* from 1905). These mythic plays involve characters waiting at a ruined site for the arrival of some spirit that might relieve them of a burden, whether it be a crime, an inherited infirmity, or the past in general. The more historically and socially grounded, but no less stylized, Dublin Trilogy of Sean O'Casey also impacted the younger writer when it was first staged in the 1920s at the Abbey Theatre, the National Theatre of Ireland. From a certain angle, the closing moments of *Juno and the Paycock* (1924) could foreshadow the tramps of Beckett's later days. Here two quixotic drunks return to an apartment emptied of furniture and family, singing on in grotesque camaraderie and oblivious to the tragedy that unfolded in their absence.

But Beckett had a complicated relationship with his birthplace. After a first stint in Paris, he had returned to Ireland to lecture in French at his Alma Mater, but quit the position a year later. After the sudden death of his father in 1933, Beckett left Ireland and, following some time in London and Germany, spent the remainder of his life in France. A voluntary exile, like Joyce and a long line of Irish writers before him, Beckett thought Ireland's conservatism and cultural remove at odds with his literary ambitions. Indeed, his work often ran afoul with the Irish censors and for a time he refused to allow productions of his plays in the country. Hard as it is to fathom, even *Krapp's Last Tape* was deemed unacceptably lewd. The

Irish censors, alert to phantoms of sexuality, absurdly charged that the reference to how the girl in the punt "let me in" referred to intercourse and demanded it be cut. As we will discuss below, the line at issue clearly speaks to the vulnerable link drawn by a shared gaze, but puritanical authorities thought otherwise.

The writer's profound influence on Irish drama has been explored at length elsewhere, but for our purposes it is worth noting that a distinct sub-genre of Irish drama beginning in the 1960s and still in evidence today seems to intersect directly with Beckett's monologues, perhaps most prominently *Krapp's Last Tape*. In Brian Friel's *Faith Healer* (1979), Mark O'Rowe's *Howie the Rookie* (1999) or *Terminus* (2007), or any of Conor McPherson's early plays, lone (often male) figures take turns retelling intertwined – at times conflicting – versions of the same event from the past. These plays find ironic pleasure in revealing the fictional nature of all memory, as we in the audience begin to recognize the lacunae in each account as the crux of the speaker's traumatic unraveling. Perhaps even more directly intertwined with Krapp's concerns with memory are plays like Tom Murphy's *Bailegangaire* (1980) or Sebastian Barry's *Steward of Christendom* (1995), where elderly characters, isolated in their past, struggle to finish narrating their history in order to arrive at a complete sense of self.

In the decades following his move to France, Beckett would only rarely return to Ireland, primarily to visit his widowed mother. Though they had a strained relationship, her death in 1950 devastated the author. It is worth noting, then, that the 27- or 29-year-old Krapp recounts "the last illness of his father" in his yearly summary while the 39-year-old Krapp focuses the first part of his narrative on his mother's death. (Since each tape circles around a death, perhaps the

69-year-old's tape implies his own impending death.) Beckett himself was 27 when his father died and 44 when his mother died – a comparable span of time, if not exactly parallel.

The "house on the canal where mother lay a-dying, in the late autumn, after her long viduity" (221) was the Merrion Nursing Home in Dublin, overlooking the Grand Canal. Beckett stayed with his mother during her final days and, as Knowlson writes, "when he could no longer bear to watch her suffer, [he would] walk disconsolately alone along the towpath of the Grand Canal" (Knowlson 1996, 345–346). A friend who lives along the canal at this very block tells me that one can still see the window of number 21 Herbert Street from Baggott Street Bridge, which crosses the Grand Canal. Looking out to that window, one can imagine Beckett (and his shadow self, Krapp) still clutching that hard rubber ball as a small white dog whimpers for attention. That Krapp admits he sat "in the biting wind, wishing she were gone" (221) may not be a confession of Beckett's own sentiments towards his own mother, but it certainly evokes the regret that, according to Knowlson's biography, he carried with him long after her passing.

We find traces of Krapp's other loves in Beckett's past. The Bianca referenced by the youngest Krapp recalls Bianca Esposito, Beckett's Italian tutor while he was a student. She was much older than he and the two were never involved romantically, but she instigated his interest in Dante (see Knowlson 1996, 67–68). But it was another unrequited love that inspired the most lyrical section of the short play. In December 1957, the same month he heard Pat Magee's BBC recording that would inspire the composition of *Krapp*, Beckett received word that his first love, Ethna McCarthy, had been diagnosed with terminal cancer. Beckett had met Ethna in his first year

of university, where her outgoing independence and flirta-
tiousness, her intelligence and marked beauty had struck the
shy and withdrawn young man deeply. In words that recall
Krapp's lingering reference to the eyes of a woman from his
past, one of Beckett's friends, Georges Pelorson, described
how Ethna "had a very beautiful face, lovely eyes, extraordi-
nary eyes – very penetrating, very sagacious and almost black"
(Knowlson 1996, 74). Though this love was never consum-
mated, the two maintained contact and Beckett remained
deeply enamored with Ethna even as the decades passed.
Knowlson speculates that "the young Beckett had consider-
able difficulty in reconciling the lusts of the flesh with the
yearnings of the spirit. Perhaps more than anything, Ethna
represented for him a glimpse of a possible harmony of flesh
and spirit, in which the loved one could be both desired and
admired at the same time" (Knowlson 1996, 75). Clearly this
meeting of opposites speaks to Krapp's own conflict between
the sensual and the ideal that we will discuss below.

It seems that memories of Ethna in her youth and the
prospect of her imminent death haunted Beckett during the
composition of *Krapp's Last Tape*. Until her death a year and
a half later, Beckett would write her long letters, full of feeling; in one of these, composed soon after he finished the play,
he clearly marked the connection between Krapp's love for
the girl on the punt and his own affection for Ethna: "I've
written in English a stage monologue for Pat Magee which
I think you will like if no one else" (Knowlson 1996, 398).

Perhaps because of its uncharacteristically personal nature,
Beckett felt especially affectionate towards the play. He wrote
to his friend Barney Rosset, "I feel as clucky and beady and
one-legged and bare-footed about this little text as an old
hen with her last chick" (Knowlson 1996, 399). But, let me

underline the fact that a comparison between the two lives, factual and fictional, can only take us so far. It does bring us closer to the issues at the heart of the play – asking us to consider how our remembered selves and the narratives we tell about our pasts intersect with the present – but it does not "solve" the play in any way, explain Beckett, or explain Krapp.

Beckett's writings remind us again and again of the fictional nature of any such narrative. We might think of *Endgame*, the play that immediately preceded the writing of *Krapp* and with which it was paired in its premiere performance in 1958. In a bunker-like dwelling, Hamm, the sovereign of a perverse and meager family/society that seems the last vestige of humanity, devotes himself to the crafting of a story that may or may not be about his past. He takes such pleasure in shaping the narrative – constantly revising the description of the weather on the day his story begins, for example – that there is no anchor upon which to ground the factual. He relishes his choice of certain words over others in much the same way that Krapp seemingly crafts his account. Ham actor that he is, prone to theatrical melodrama, Hamm wants to be seen and heard.

Or, we might think of the character Moran, ostensibly the writer and protagonist of the novel *Molloy*. He concludes his text with the following lines: "It is midnight. The rain is beating on the windows. It was not midnight. It was not raining" (Beckett 2010a, 170). All statements from such a writer are doubled by an equally valid contradiction.

And so I must confess I'm not telling the entire truth either. I could not find my tape and its companions, for I discovered that nearly all of these recordings had been thrown out many years ago or had been converted into a digital format. The critic Steven Connor writes about how Beckett's language has a way of infecting those who dwell with it too long. These elliptical phrases that suspend the weight of specific reference, they pass between reader and writer like the stones that Molloy sucks over and over and passes from pocket to pocket, until he cannot remember which came first and where. Vivian Mercier likewise claims that interpretations of Beckett's work "reveal more about the psyches of the people who offer them than about the work itself or the psyche of its author" (Mercier 1977, vii). I dream myself as Krapp, echo his lines, and find myself dreading his arrival. Even as I write these words, I am sitting in my own little studio at the top floor of a house on the outskirts of town, a single lamp lit on my desk. I will occasionally step off into the dark to fill a glass of wine or a tumbler of bourbon, lubricants to the words that may come. I will sing to myself. And I, too, find myself lingering on the eyes of lovers past, flipping through pages of old diaries, old photographs. I seem to play the same part that Krapp did, coming back to this desk to write this book or its correlate, words no one may read. This is the slow undertow of Beckett's writing – take care lest it pull you under as well.

3

How it happens

What kind of a play is this? A tragedy or a comedy? Is Krapp some great, broken man, a king dethroned, or is he simply an old fool? Are we meant to pity him or despise him, weep for him or laugh at him? If I propose these as choices between opposing extremities of reaction, I am only mimicking the terms that the play offers. Beckett structures *Krapp's Last Tape* around a series of binary oppositions, and holds them in delicate balance throughout. I'm in agreement with the critic David H. Hesla, who wrote that throughout Beckett's art, "optimism and pessimism, hope and despair, comedy and tragedy are counterbalanced by one another: none of them is allowed to become an Absolute" (Hesla 1971, 215). Accordingly, in this section we'll trace out a few of these opposing terms; but just as Krapp cannot find reconciliation between these forms, we too will keep ourselves unsettled.

Critics and artists have debated over the definition of tragedy for millennia, though some general characteristics run through these many understandings. Usually a tragedy centers upon a single protagonist whose expression of free will, freedom, or ambition bring forth unintended consequences that ultimately lead to his or her downfall. In its classical iteration, this hero must begin at some social and moral height in order to descend a great distance by the play's end. Think of the quintessentially tragic Oedipus, beginning the play as the city's ruler and savior, but discovering by the end of Sophocles's *Oedipus Rex* that he has unknowingly killed his father, married his mother, and given birth to his siblings. His mother/wife kills herself; he blinds himself, and is exiled from the city. Its hard to imagine falling a greater distance than that.

Such characteristics pose problems for Beckettian characters. Most of these tramp-like or abandoned figures have the slightest of aspirations – they may seek relief or an end to their world, they may seek a reason or task from their absent master (*Waiting for Godot*), relief from their present master (*Endgame*), or a return to their mother without quite knowing why (*Molloy*), but they do not seek a beginning or to create anew. They await deliverance. Krapp is a different animal – at least in his earlier incarnation, where he desires greatness as a writer. Ostensibly, he has free will and a mobility that, however compromised, could allow him movements impossible for most of Beckett's other characters. And yet habit has so confined Krapp to a pattern of behavior that we might say he has been fated to repeat himself *ad nauseum*. No longer living in the shadow of those jealous gods from classical tragedy, if there is a tragic curse laid upon Krapp it is one that has been invoked by that most ubiquitous of gods: Habit. For, as Leonard C. Pronko has written, "the tragedy of Krapp, and of all men in Beckett's view, is not that we become what we were not, but that we are now and evermore the same" (Pronko 1962, 51). Or, as Beckett puts it in his book on Proust: "Habit is the ballast that chains the dog to his vomit" (Beckett 1989, 19).

Nothing happens once for Krapp. His entire life is built around habits and repetitions: his yearly birthday ritual that begins alone in the Winehouse and ends with his new recording of his old year, his habitual drinking (his statistical analysis of his time spent in bars: "seventeen hundred hours, out of the preceding eight thousand odd, consumed on licensed premises alone" [220]), his abandoned loves whom he repeatedly sees as distractions from the work he should be doing. Consider the title of the play in full – *Krapp's Last Tape: A Play in One Act*. Bernard Dukore ruminates on the double meaning of the subtitle's "One Act," which not only refers to the structure of the short play, but also "suggests that all of Krapp's tape recording sessions are ultimately the same, are essentially one act" (Dukore 1973, 351). This is not to say that he does nothing, but rather that Krapp repeatedly decides *not to do something* for the future – to commit to love. As Paul Lawley suggests, the memories that Krapp rehearses, "whether bright or miserable, are not just images of the past but regretful intimations of a future he might have had" if only he had chosen differently (Lawley 2015, 374).

Classical tragedy relies upon the tragic protagonist experiencing a moment of recognition in which he or she fully grasps the irrevocable consequences of his or her actions. As written, Krapp does not seem to come to terms with himself, though one might make the case that the lastness of this particular tape suggests otherwise. Perhaps his sudden wrenching of the reel from the machine in the midst of recording his current year signals some decision to abort the habitual cycle? In certain productions, this moment appears irrevocably destructive, preventing him from recording another tape afterwards, even if he wanted to do so. Does he realize the intensely bitter irony in the last words of the middle-aged

Krapp? "Perhaps my best years are gone. When there was a chance of happiness. But I wouldn't want them back. Not with the fire in me now. No, I wouldn't want them back" (226). Perhaps his final frozen stare as the tape plays out and the lights dim signals some unspoken recognition. We in the audience clearly see his doomed situation.

It is easy to fall into sentimentality here, to feel nothing but pity for this old man as he looks back on a life of disappointment. Conscientious of this temptation, Beckett worked to balance the impulses towards the maudlin with a more comedic character. The opening moments of the play – when Krapp eats his two bananas and shuffles about the stage, fumbling over objects – resemble a slapstick pantomime. It recalls the silent opening of *Endgame*, in which a limping Clov clomps about his bunker, setting the stage for the performance that will follow. Both "preshows" present their characters as rather ungainly stagehands awkwardly prepping the spectacle that will follow. No theatrical magic here or anonymous technicians in black seamlessly working the ropes. These are rather ridiculous men, fussing about in the half-light as they have on many other occasions.

From the start, then, Beckett establishes an ambivalent picture of Krapp. This is apparent in the costume of the man standing there onstage. As discussed above, the stage directions describe a Krapp in ill-fitting clothes with the whitish face and purple nose of a circus clown or a cartoonish heavy drinker, though even the original production ignored the last of these characteristics. In later productions that Beckett advised and directed, he would further soften the exaggeratedly clownlike appearance, changing the white boots for dark slippers that made a shuffling sound, replacing the shortened trousers with a pair that were slightly too long, as if Krapp were shrinking with age (see Knowlson 1992). He retained the clownlike elements of the character's physical movements, however: the repetitive gestures that approached the mechanistic. In this way, he maintained the comic elements in the role since, as the philosopher Henri Bergson writes, "*the attitudes, gestures and movements of the human body are laughable in exact proportion as that body reminds us of a mere machine*" (Bergson 1911, 15; original italics).

It is difficult, too, to take a character called Krapp too seriously. His very name is a rather crude scatological joke on his lasting "condition" as he puts it. His youngest self bemoans his "unattainable laxation" (220); his middle-aged self deems his penchant for bananas "fatal things for a man with my condition" (219); and his eldest self laments "the sour cud and the iron stool" (224) that remain his constant companions. In short, Krapp has difficulty crapping, but no difficulty passing the hot air of words. This constipation afflicts both his body and his work: he cannot produce writing, or what little he does produce is also impacted and does not circulate – "seventeen copies sold" (224) of his magnum opus. It travels about as far as he does in his rare and meager outings – "Crawled out once or twice, before the summer was cold" (224).

In other words, as with many of Beckett's plays and prose writings, *Krapp* is caught between tragic and comedic expectations. That tension seems fundamental to the drive of the piece – its humor tenderizes our attention, makes us vulnerable to the poignancy and horror of Krapp's situation. How much more painful to see the absurdity of our own habitual actions, how pathetic they appear from without? We could find some consolation in the nobility of our suffering if we could rise to the state of tragic greatness, but we can only play out a dumb slapstick routine.

The dualism that undergirds the play most clearly is the dichotomy between the dark and the light, the black and white. This opposition is apparent in the very image of the stage from the outset. There he stands with white face, shirt, and shocking white boots, but otherwise dressed in "rusty" black clothing. The light over his desk keeps at bay the midnight darkness that surrounds. Apart from a blush of red, a bit of phallic yellow skin protruding from a pocket, he appears a portrait in black and white.

This dichotomy recurs often throughout the text of the play, too, where Krapp knowingly refers to the light and the dark as the terms through which he knows his world – "everything on this old muckball, all the light and the dark ..." (224) – and it marks those encounters that matter most to him. To mention only the black aspect: there is the black plumage of the vidua bird, the black ball, the black perambulator, and so on. He also enacts that meeting between light and dark repeatedly over the course of his years. His epiphany occurs on the equinox – the day when the length of night and day are equal – before a lighthouse on the edge of a storm-tossed night, a kind of outdoor reiteration of the beacon-like stage picture we see before us. He tells of sitting before the luminous fire at the Winehouse with eyes closed, making his own darkness in the face of light. There is even the name of Miss McGlome, the occasional singer downstairs, which recalls the "gloaming," another word for dusk.

Krapp's great conflict revolves around the fact that he feels driven to keep these opposing terms separate from one another, to structure an order out of the chaos of experience. And yet, each of the three significant events in the 39-year-old's account occupies a moment of transition (death, revelation, and departure), in a place where opposites meet: at

the water's edge. His mother's death witnessed from the weir
(a stone embankment across a river), his epiphany at the end
of the jetty, and his farewell to love on the punt – each a limi-
nal place between land and sea.

Beckett emphasizes this dichotomy in his own later reflec-
tions on the play. The notebook that the playwright prepared when he first came to direct the work more than ten
years after its premiere devotes several pages to the matter, listing the instances of light and dark throughout the
play as structural features. His notes here go to some length
exploring the Manichean aspects of the piece, an analysis
to which scholars have devoted no small attention. Beckett
would emphasize that this reading came to him only with
the distance of years, that this had not been a conscious
principle at the time of writing and does not offer some
consummate meaning to the play. As such, I will only sum-
marize here where interested readers might delve further
(Knowlson 1992, xxi–xxv).

Manicheism is a fourth-century branch of gnostic faith,
whose adherents believed the world was divided between the
dark (matter) and the light (spirit). According to Beckett, "the
duty of reason being not to join but to separate" (Knowlson
1992, 141), practitioners pursued this separation by avoiding
the material or sensual in favor of the spiritual. They sought
an "ascetic ethics, particularly abstinence from sensual enjoy-
ment. Sexual desire, marriage, forbidden (signaculum sinus)
[taboo on sex]" (Knowlson 1992, 137). Of course, Krapp's life
is convoluted with desires of the flesh – for sex, for drink, for
a banana – but he berates himself for these inclinations.

Even without aligning this dualism with Manichean faith,
for Beckett-the-director and for any design team that might
tackle the piece today the opposition between light and dark

offers a strong visual language for approaching a production. For Krapp has fashioned his surroundings to this measure: "the new light above my table is a great improvement. With all this darkness round me I feel less alone. [. . .] I love to get up and move about in it, then back here to . . . (*hesitates*) . . . me. (*Pause.*) Krapp" (219). And so, the light seems to represent Krapp himself, the darkness posing a loss of self that nonetheless offers some comfort in its surrounding otherness. At least as written in the original script, the drink with its promise of abandonment hides in that darker recess. Charles R. Lyons poses that "rather than the opposition of public and private, interior and exterior, Beckett establishes a conflict between antithetical desires: to lose the self in darkness and to confront the self in the light" (Lyons 1983, 101). We might then connect the light with the analytic attention of reason, clarity, and individualism and the dark with the sensual, the undifferentiated, the interpersonal – what Friedrich Nietzsche would term the Apollonian and the Dionysian respectively in his 1872 book *The Birth of Tragedy from the Spirit of Music*.

It is in his relationships with women that Krapp most often confronts his anxiety around differentiation. We are told that the youngest Krapp lived "on and off with Bianca [Italian for white] in Kedar Street [Hebrew for black]" (220) – *on and off*, in oscillation, but never consistently. There is the dark nurse in stark white wheeling her black pram, at first meeting his gaze in seeming interest and then threatening to call the police at his approach. And, most movingly, there are the dark eyes of the woman on the punt, set against the bright light of a sun so blinding he must shift the cast of his shadow to allow her eyes to open. She "lets him in," but only in order that they might say farewell. Even Krapp's mother's death is signaled by a lowered blind, an act shutting out the light.

Why is Krapp so consumed with the look of these different women throughout his past, pausing in particular on the eyes of each? The middle Krapp summarizes the youngest Krapp's tape about living with Bianca as recounting "not much about her, apart from a tribute to her eyes. Very warm. I suddenly saw them again" (220). Later he himself recalls the "dark beauty" with the perambulator outside his mother's hospital, who had her eyes on him – green eyes, "like chrysolite!" (222). And then there are the eyes of the girl on the punt.

Looking into another's eyes, one is, as Krapp has it, "let in" to that other's being. Or, as Elaine Scarry rather strikingly puts it, "no wonder it is overwhelming to look into another person's eyes; one beholds directly the moist tissue of the person's brain" (Scarry 2001, 68). And to be seen by another – to be *really* seen – is to be invited into a shared co-presence.

Torn as always between opposing intentions, Krapp wants to recede into solitude away from the eyes of others, yet, contrarily, whatever desire he feels towards these women revolves around the promise that he might be recognized by their attention. Here, he belongs to a long line of Beckettian characters who seek confirmation of their existence in the acknowledgment of another. In *Play*, for example, the trio entombed in urns are damned to repeat the narrative of their past in purgatorial endlessness, without response from any other apart from the spotlight that hails them to perform their role. "Am I as much as . . . being seen?" one wonders (Beckett 2010b, 160). Beckett would often refer to the eighteenth-century Irish philosopher George Berkeley's claim that "to be is to be perceived," such that a tree does not fall in the woods unless there is someone there to witness the event. Applied to the self, one's existence hinges on the fact of another's perception. Indeed, when Vladimir asks the boy to deliver a message to the invisible Godot at the end of *Waiting for Godot*, he merely requests, "tell him . . . (*he hesitates*) . . . tell him you saw me and that . . . (*he hesitates*) . . . that you saw me" (Beckett 2010b, 82).

Other characters in Beckett's world flee from perception, much as Krapp recedes into his dark chamber above the world and leaves behind his trail of lovers. *Film* (1965), Beckett's lone work for the cinema, is essentially one long chase scene in which the great silent film actor Buster Keaton (performing in his last film role) flees all forms of perception – those of strangers and neighbors, dogs and fish, even the eyes of people in photographs. Of course, as long as the film is playing, he cannot escape the camera's perception. But it is only at the end of the film that the spectator discovers that the camera is in fact the character's own self-perception, an eye that he cannot avoid as long as he is conscious. As Beckett once said in an interview, "self-perception is the most frightening of all human observations . . . when man faces himself he is looking into the abyss" (Mercier 1977, 4).

If *Film* is, as its title claims, about the medium of film, the conflict between perception and self-perception presents a different problem in the theatre, where characters onstage may share a common time and space with that silent mass of voyeurs sitting in the dark, but often must not know that co-presence entirely. The world on one side of the invisible barrier cannot intercede on behalf of the world on the other side, even as each requires the other to sustain the life of the performance. Beckett interrogates this theatrical conundrum in a number of his plays, where the characters obliquely reference the audience without directly seeing them, often to comedic effect. (Witness, for example, Clov turning his telescope to face the audience and crying out, "I see . . . a multitude . . .

in transports . . . of joy" [Beckett 2010b, 110].) The published playscript of *Krapp's Last Tape* signals an awareness of this theatrical divide between the stage world and the "real" world of the audience when, after slipping on the first banana peel, Krapp nudges the skin over the edge of the stage into the pit. Beckett was seemingly uncomfortable with the way in which this comedic action broke the fourth wall of the stage, that illusory skin separating our bodies from those onstage; beginning with his own production of the play in 1969 and with all subsequent performances in which he was involved, Krapp would discard the peel into the darkness off to the side of the stage instead of transgressing into the audience's domain. Thus, the limits of the stage world were retained and Krapp could continue on alone.

Arguably, Krapp records himself for another to hear him, to perceive that he existed – whether that other is his future self or some imagined archivist, seeking material on the great writer he would become. I'm ashamed to say that, when I was younger (very young, I promise!) I wrote in my journal with this latter intent lurking at the back of my mind. I wished that my forthcoming "great work" would send researchers poring over handwritten notes for clues to my compositions. Or I worried that a future child might come across those scrawls and see me there. This self-construction encouraged the artful phrase, the discrete oversight surrounding whatever compromising situation – no stupidity, no sex, and only an appropriately romantic malaise. And even if we write only for ourselves, we must wonder: which self? The self now, the one tomorrow, or the hypothetical sixty-nine-year-old self that we hope to become? Or the one we fear we will? Who is this hypothetical reader or listener "some late evening in the future"?

These recordings are a way of seeing the self as another. Krapp always speaks of his younger self in the third person: middle Krapp refers to youngest Krapp as "he," and eldest Krapp, in turn, refers to middle Krapp as "he." Using grammar to distance himself from his past may allow Krapp to laugh at, or comment on, that earlier self, but it also allows him to appear as a character. He is seen; he exists as a separate and contained entity. Wayne Koestenbaum suggests that "recording your voice, the talking machine seemed to be *listening* to you. A confessional, it absorbed your secrets, stored them, and replayed them" (Koestenbaum 2001, 50). If the machine listens to you, then you have something interesting to say, and there is a "you" that might be constituted out of the tangle of memories and emotions.

In Krapp's case, the self-as-other is nonetheless a rather repugnant production. Following a rather crude psychoanalytic reading, let me point out how defecation produces a separate entity from the self – the crap – that was only recently a part of the subject. The *Oxford English Dictionary* tells us that an obsolete meaning of the word "crap" was "the husk of grain; chaff" and traces the etymology of the word to the "rejected or left matter, residue, dregs, dust." Krapp seems to know as much when his middle self speaks of sitting before the fire at the Winehouse, preparing for the evening's recording and "separating the grain from the husk" (219).

What is it that remains from this mania for separation, these many oppositions and distinctions? Krapp ruminates further that the grain might be "those things worth having when all the dust has – when all *my* dust has settled," by which the middle Krapp means his "great work." Of course, for the elder the roles have been reversed; he now sees his work as the husk and his abandoned loves as the grain worth having. (How fitting that he loves the banana, that fruit to be peeled, separated, husked, with such ease.) But in carrying a name that means "husk of grain," Krapp is and becomes the thing that remains apart from the memorable, the worthwhile. If a name dictates a fated course, then the old gods of tragedy could not be more cruel than whoever has burdened Krapp with this cursed name. And the gods of comedy could not have arrived at a crueler joke.

4

When it happens

In a remarkable early essay on *Waiting for Godot*, the French novelist Alain Robbe-Grillet describes how Beckett's characters are staked to the present moment in a way that touches on the essential nature of the theatre as an artform:

> The human condition, Heidegger says, is *to be there*. Probably it is the theatre, more than any other mode of representing reality, which reproduces this situation most naturally. The dramatic character is on stage, that is his primary quality: he is there.
>
> (Robbe-Grillet 1965, 111)

He is there, on the other side of that invisible barrier that divides the stage world from those of us watching, but he is also here and now, with us. In other words, he appears in our presence and in our present moment. Krapp begins his play staring front in silence, looking into the empty common time and space that we share, and then checking his watch, as if to make sure that the time is correct, that we are all ready to begin, here and now.

And yet, this present is clearly not the only time at work in this performance, so bound as it is to the past, or any performance for that matter. In his book *The Haunted Stage: Theatre as a Memory Machine*, the scholar Marvin Carlson reminds us that, even as the theatre is always concerned with witnessing in the present moment, it finds itself constantly glancing backward:

> The close association of the theatre with the evocation of the past, the histories and legends of the culture uncannily restored to a mysterious half-life here, has made the theatre in the minds of many the art most closely related to memory and the theatre building itself a kind of memory machine.
>
> (Carlson 2002, 142)

The stage swells with ghosts – sometimes quite literally, as in Hamlet's nightly apparition, or Krapp's youthful recording, but also in the eerie "half-life" of any character who appears onstage, revived every night to play out the same events in their scant lifespan. For Carlson and others, the theatre is haunted by prior performances, by all the actors who played whatever role in previous productions, and by all the rehearsals that led to the event that seems to be happening for the first time here and now. And so Krapp finds himself playing with one memory machine (the tape recorder) in the heart of another, far older, memory machine (the theatre).

The material representation of this repetitive course is the tape itself, looping back from one reel to another in a winding and unwinding of time. Tape is, in the words of Steven Connor, "the medium that most seems to embody the predicament of temporal embodiment – by linking us to our losses, making it possible for us to recall what we can no longer remember, keeping us in touch with what nevertheless remains out of reach, making us remain what we no longer are" (Connor 2014, 101). There is a contradiction at the heart of the recording, with its desire to keep a thing that is not to be held and resounds only in its passage. "Sound exists only when it is going out of existence," Walter Ong writes in his seminal book *Orality and Literacy: the Technologizing of the Word*: "[i]t is not simply perishable but essentially evanescent, and it is sensed as evanescent" (Ong 1982, 32). In this, sound possesses a common root with performance, for we might say that live performance itself (and life for that matter) is "essentially evanescent," always on its way away.

For Krapp, the tape recorder becomes not only an extension of his memory, but an extension of his body; he relates to it as if it were another character, by turns cursing and caressing it. Later, listening to the episode on the punt, he draws it close, encircles his arms about its form as if it took the place of the lover that is gone, reflecting what Beckett names in his production notebook the "[t]endency of a solitary person to enjoy affective relationships with objects" (Knowlson 1992, 205). The playwright Edward Albee remembers how, in the German premiere production in 1959, a loudspeaker was placed on the stage to play the tapes and, during the punt sequence at the end, "this actor playing Krapp got up from behind his desk, took his chair, went and sat by this huge loudspeaker, and put his arms around it. It was beautiful, totally beautiful" (Knowlson 1980, 230). If there is an erotics here, it is one in keeping with the fact of listening itself, for hearing weaves the world and listener into one, threaded through portals we can block, but cannot close. "Sight isolates, sound incorporates," writes Ong, "whereas sight situates the observer outside what he views, at a distance, sound pours into the hearer" (Ong 1982, 72). More than sight might allow, in hearing one's past, one becomes a part of that past.

Some of this physical connection perhaps derives from the fact that these are analogue recordings, that they hold a material imprint in their very fiber. In its substance and surface, the tape retains so much more than simple speech – silence and hesitation, as well as all the detritus surrounding an enunciation, the stutters and thickenings of a voice, a throat closing up on itself. The mechanics of these particular tapes deserve attention, since we no longer make use of such technology in this digital age. Each spool is a single reel of magnetic tape, which is mounted on the machine's spindle and then manually threaded into a second empty "takeup reel." As the tape plays it uncoils from one reel and coils about the other – one diminishing, as the other grows large. In a sense, then, each reel functions like the opposing globes of an hourglass. Both time-measuring devices contain a fixed past duration; like the sand in an hourglass, the matter contained inside the tape remains impervious to change. One can stop the motion, perhaps turn it back, but it exists in a separate time from that of the person who manipulates it.

I say impervious, but that isn't entirely true. Tapes have become quite obsolete, muted into silence when phased out of production – note the boxes of cassettes that were discarded from my childhood home. Moreover, tape decays as it is played; the very act of running it through a machine's tape head wears it away, distorts its playing. Think of William Basinski's devastating musical work *The Disintegration Loops*. In the 1980s, the experimental composer had crafted short tape loops from found pieces of innocuous easy-listening music – each sample no more than a few seconds long; when he tried to transfer the music from tape to digital recording decades later, he discovered that the material was decaying as it passed repeatedly over the head. Over tracks running up to an hour in length, *The Disintegration Loops* collect a churning heave of sound as it leaves us in cracks and rustles, clusters of dust made audible and then emptying out to silence, through countless repetitions. The story goes that Basinski finished his recording on the morning of September 11, 2001, and sat atop the roof of his New York apartment building filming the smoke as it rose from the great ruins downtown. Later he would lay his decaying music over the silent film of those other collapsing materialities, twin departures suspended in the seeming eternity of digital stasis.

Is this how time wears away at memory, the rehearsal of our wounds and wonders continuously peeling off from the original experience in words that fit less and less? In spite of Krapp's attempts, his grasp on the past has turned feeble. He puzzles over each line in the ledger's description of his thirty-ninth year, answering the entry "Equinox, memorable equinox" with a puzzled and humorously ironic "Memorable equinox?" Where the middle Krapp attaches significance to the ball he gives to the dog, his elder listener cannot place the object. No matter how hard he tries to put words to this kernel of memory – calls it "old, black, hard, solid" – no matter how he thinks that "I shall feel it, in my hand, until my dying day," his older self cannot remember its singularity. It means nothing to him when he reads of it in his ledger ("The black ball . . . [*He raises his head, stares blankly front. Puzzled.*] Black ball?"). Even the break in the final line of the written record, "Farewell to – (*He turns the page*) – love" (219), suggests that he cannot quite recall to what he bid farewell. This difference between the past recorded and the past experienced is clearly at issue in a play divided between disembodied speaker and embodied listener.

Beckett knew all of this quite well. He had studied it and written of it in the single book he wrote during his brief career as an academic. This short, quite brilliant volume on the French novelist Marcel Proust, titled simply *Proust* (1931), resembles the occasional pieces of art criticism he would write throughout his life, in that it reflects as much on his own aesthetics as it does on that of his purported subject. (Like many of us, when Beckett wrote about others, he was really writing about himself.) Proust's seven-volume masterpiece, *In Search of Lost Time*, is itself semi-autobiographical and, like *Krapp's Last Tape*, concerns time and memory, first and foremost. Beckett's study quotes from the ending of the novel:

> I would describe men, even at the risk of giving them the appearance of monstrous beings, as occupying in Time a much greater place than that so sparingly conceded to them in Space, a place indeed extended beyond measure, because, like giants plunged in the years, they touch at once those periods of their lives – separated by so many days – so far apart in Time.
>
> (Beckett 1989, 12)

Krapp, too, extends far beyond the small cone of light within which he labors, far beyond the small and shriveled frame of a man curled over his recording. Much as a tape unwound extends a greater distance than its spool takes up, Krapp is a "giant plunged in the years." This giant's form unfurls through the memories he speaks and those to which he listens.

Beckett describes two different modes of memory that Proust explores in his writing. The first, voluntary memory is memory that is already known and already processed by our intelligence. It does not touch upon the unwieldy complexity of reality, but gives us a story or sketch of reality in a hand we recognize as our own. Voluntary memory is fixed and ordered by cause and effect like lines on a ledger, arranged in our mental archive and available for recall. Krapp's attempts at recording, boxing, and then summarizing his past in his ledgerbook seek to neatly contain all experience within voluntary recall. For they do not retain authentic lived contact with what has happened; rather they tell stories about his previous year, frame events in words. He holds his tapes in much the same way that Beckett's other characters hoard their meager possessions: as markers of their self and its limits. In *Malone Dies*, for example, the eponymous bedbound protagonist enumerates his belongings like characteristics of his person, encircling them in his arms and clutching them close as if to incorporate them into his very constitution.

Involuntary memory, on the other hand, is unruly and untamed, beyond our beck and call. It appears on its own, triggered by some peripheral and overlooked aspect of the original past reality. In the most famous example from Proust's novel, the narrator tastes a *petite madeleine* cake soaked in tea and finds himself suddenly consumed by an indescribable joy as the memory of eating such a cake as a child arises unbidden. Suddenly, the whole panorama of that time and place unfolds before him, as it was experienced, not as it was named or told. Incidentally, it is such an imaginary memory that actors seek to employ in sensory recall, when, by attending to some atmospheric quality, a past emotion is brought into the present. Set in motion by such an involuntary trigger, Beckett writes, "the total past sensation, not its echo nor its copy, but the sensation itself, annihilating every spatial and temporal restriction, comes in a rush to engulf the subject in all the beauty of its infallible proportion" (Beckett 1989, 72).

Framing Krapp in this light shows us that his seeming mania for recording the past might – like everything in his life – pull in two different directions at once. On one hand, he may intend to control or limit the past's presence, to process it and let it lie in its proper reel and box – the archive of voluntary memory. To remember in this manner is a way of disarming the past's hold on the present self, to digest its impression by making it part of a story told. Here, hopefully, one sets the past aside in order to live a present that looks out towards the future unburdened.

On the other hand, it seems that Krapp wants to return to the past itself, though he knows, in some way, that the record will not evoke that distant experience, that he must look elsewhere for its piercing touch. When he finally abandons his recording of the current year, pulling the tape from the machine in what seems an irrevocable refusal of the archival impulse, Krapp tellingly admits that he will soon go to bed to:

> lie propped up in the dark – and wander. Be again in the dingle on a Christmas Eve, gathering holly, the red-berried. [. . .] Be again, be again. (*Pause.*) All that old misery. (*Pause.*) Once wasn't enough for you. (*Pause.*) Lie down across her.
>
> (225)

The machine of memory does not bring back the "old misery" of living, which instead arises in bedbound reverie. Was Krapp miserable in the midst of living those far-fetched memories that he now craves so, or does the misery arrive because they are no longer here, offering their many possible futures?

At the same time that Krapp's scission from the present
traps him in the past, it also sees him leaning into the future.
The pacing of the performance itself mimics these divergent
orientations of Krapp's attention. Under the searching beam
of a lighthouse, Krapp has what could be described as a reali-
zation of creative empowerment, told in a passionate drive
onward that is ironically reasserted in the elder Krapp's impa-
tient desire to skip over this same section. That frantic and
forceful expression cuts away to the diametrically opposed
calm of the scene on the punt. The recorded Krapp has settled
into a lyrical and flowing language that, in mimic of the boat
ride he describes, catches intermittently on shoals of silence.
Indulge me as I quote this beautiful passage at length:

> . . . upper lake, with the punt, bathed off the bank, then
> pushed out into the stream and drifted. She lay stretched
> out on the floorboards with her hands under her head and
> her eyes closed. Sun blazing down, bit of a breeze, water
> nice and lively. I noticed a scratch on her thigh and asked
> her how she came by it. Picking gooseberries, she said.
> I said again I thought it was hopeless and no good going
> on, and she agreed, without opening her eyes. (*Pause.*)
> I asked her to look at me and after a few moments –
> (*pause*) – after a few moments she did, but the eyes just
> slits, because of the glare. I bent over her to get them in the
> shadow and they opened. (*Pause. Low.*) Let me in. (*Pause.*)
> We drifted in among the flags and stuck. The way they
> went down, sighing, before the stem! (*Pause.*) I lay down
> across her with my face in her breasts and my hand on her.
> We lay there without moving. But under us all moved, and
> moved us, gently, up and down, and from side to side.
>   (223)

Where he can only imagine a common time with his mother from afar via the mediation of a canine other ("Her moments, my moments. (*Pause.*) The dog's moments" [222]), on the punt the back and forth of time's momentary fluctuation moves both himself and his lover in a shared passage, "gently, up and down, and from side to side." If the dog stands in as a surrogate for the shared moments with his mother that he cannot endure, then here Krapp appears in a rare instance of connection with another person. Yet even as the two may lie still together, suspended in an oceanic stasis at the peak of summer (gooseberries are usually harvested in June or July), and in perhaps the only span of conscious embrace of the present that Krapp recognizes, all the world continues apace, the day on its inevitable creep away from itself, towards the autumn. How the elder Krapp wants that punt to stay stuck in among the flags of the reeds, but how time cannot allow him that respite. The sun will sink lower, and the two will rouse themselves. They will make their way back to the landing. And they will say farewell as that time irrevocably passes. If there is truth in his claim that it is "hopeless and no good going on," then it is because this moment will be going on, will be gone. The future end looms.

For the middle-aged Krapp, this means something quite different, of course. He thinks the relationship itself pointless, and that, wed as he is to his work, he has no time to spare for another passion. Work, in these terms, is an exercise that perpetually sacrifices the present for the future; it always remains to be done. Krapp's epiphany promised that the good work could finally begin, not that it might ever be finished. And even in his eldest state, Krapp cannot let go of this thought that he might still begin once more. In fact, it is his admission that he "sometimes wondered in the night if a last effort

mightn't—" (225) that causes him to abandon his yearly recollection. If the tapes indicate how he empties the present
into the past, then the commitment to work is the mirroring
evacuation of the present into an ever-waiting future.

"Perhaps my best years are gone. When there was a chance
of happiness. But I wouldn't want them back. Not with the
fire in me now. No, I wouldn't want them back" (226). With
these ironic last lines – ironic because we know he wants
nothing more than a return to those years that were so bitter
in their living, nothing more than their chance at happiness –
Krapp anchors himself in the past and towards the future.
"The fire in me now" is no warming comfort in the present,
but a fire that would feed his future production.

As the voice dies out we watch Krapp lasting on, staring
out into the audience for some time before the lights too
fade to black. When working on the piece a decade after
the premiere, this time as a director, Beckett discovered that
the tape machine the theatre was using as a prop had a red
light that stayed lit when in use. He had the stage lights fade
to black while the red light sustained itself, like an unblink-
ing red eye staring out, as the tape reeled on in silence. The
machine appeared as some embodiment of the endlessly
present gaze of the theatre itself, as constant and unsympa-
thetic as a distant star transmitting light across the void from
another world. Cold comfort, that fire.

5

Where it happens

If this final section asks *where* Krapp happens, it considers both the composition of the stage and the many individual productions of the play since its premiere. Along the way it looks also at *who* performed the part, *how* the play was performed, and *when* it was performed – at bottom, too, *what* was performed changes with each iteration of a play. So perhaps this is a fine way to end our inquiry, by undermining the neat categories of interrogation that we have followed thus far.

Beckett only directed one play written by another author – Robert Pinget's *L'Hypothèse* – though he mounted several productions of his own work in his later years. He was closely involved with stagings of *Krapp's Last Tape* from the very beginning, and it is arguably the play to which he most frequently returned. He attended several weeks of rehearsals for the 1958 premiere at the Royal Court Theatre, where Donald McWhinnie directed Patrick Magee, and for the French premiere in 1960. He first directed the play himself in 1969 in Berlin, then again in 1975 in Paris, and in 1977 for the San Quentin Drama Workshop. A facsimile of his director's notebook was published in 1992 as part of a series edited by Knowlson, which together provide a wealth of information on the playwright's understanding of his own work. Set alongside the accounts of critics and actors, the notebook illustrates Beckett's increasing refinement of the play, less in terms of the spoken text than in the delineation of a *mise-en-scène* – the lights, set, sounds, and actions of the performance itself.

Beckett acquired a reputation for requiring that his works be performed as written, and those strictures have been reinforced by the Beckett Estate after his death. Most famously, he demanded the cancellation of a run of *Endgame* at the American Repertory Theatre in 1984 when director JoAnne Akalaitis took the play from its original spare and minimalist bunker and recast it in an elaborately designed post-apocalyptic subway station, complete with ruined train car hanging precariously overhead. She also inserted other markers of time and place, and rearranged the script to incorporate strong and jarring musical interludes (the production went ahead but the program was required to include a note by Beckett disavowing the work; see Kalb 1989, 78–87). However, as we will see below, directors and designers have been given relative free rein in their interpretation of these texts as long as these interpretations retain whatever we might assume to be Beckett's intent.

Even the first productions did not follow Beckett's stage directions word for word. I mentioned earlier how the clown-like "purple nose" (217) was toned down in the original production and in productions afterwards, and any reference to such an appearance was removed entirely from Beckett's later versions. The productions did, however, adhere to the timeless and placeless quality of the scene, and the reduced means characteristic of the playwright's minimalist aesthetic. The light under which Krapp toils and the surrounding black into which he ventures presage the later Beckett plays with their condensation of the playing space to a single image in the middle of unarticulated darkness. In seven of the plays following *Krapp's Last Tape*, Beckett explicitly states in the stage directions how, apart from the small area of action, the "rest of the stage is in darkness." (See *Play*, *Come and Go*, *Not I*, *That Time*, *Footfalls*, *Rockaby*, and *Ohio Impromptu*. The play that immediately precedes *Krapp's Last Tape*, the short mime *Act Without Words II* from 1957, is the first piece to employ this directive when describing the stage space.)

The light defines a very limited space about the figure as if to explicitly show the range of his senses and his sensible world. The younger Krapp describes a series of significant events that all take place in striking environments – in late autumn along the weir outside the hospital where his mother lies dying, at the pier in a wild nighttime storm where he has his epiphany, and then finally in the punt on the sunlit water. Each is cast in a particular exterior scene, in the shade of a distinct climate, and amidst the open expanse of a world populated with other people and what we might call nature. Now he has been reduced to the smallest interior under the constant glare of an artificial lamp. Hampered, too, by a "laborious" walk (219), Krapp's range of motion and the very extent of his world have been reduced significantly. Such confinement was not substantially altered when Beckett later added a second lit space upstage in his own productions of the play: the cubby to which Krapp frequently returns for his drinks and other supplies. This highlighted the twin anchors of his world – the vestibule for drink and the desk for work.

It is be expected, then, that Krapp's self-imposed confines would speak so clearly to other forms of isolation. An early production of *Waiting for Godot* that was performed in San Quentin State Prison by the Actor's Workshop of San Francisco famously spoke to the inmates with a clarity lost on more "sophisticated" and practiced theatregoers. Locked in his cell and forced to listen to the performance through the PA system, a prisoner named Rick Cluchey was inspired to form the San Quentin Drama Workshop, which would go on to produce a number of Beckett's plays. Cluchey recognized a profound connection between the incarceration of Beckett's characters and that of the men in the prison:

> If Krapp, as I performed him at San Quentin (in 1963), is a frustrated man, so was every convict in our audience. If Krapp seemed to reject his burden of past misery as being too heavy, so had these poor, bitter convicts! "All the dead voices," a line from *Godot*, seems to speak of the situation Krapp is in. He is trying to redeem time, the lost time, his past time; and so were the convicts. [. . .] At San Quentin, Krapp was in a trap; but then so was the audience.
>
> (Knowlson 1980, 197)

Years after the prison production of the play, and after Cluchey's life sentence for robbery and kidnapping had been commuted to life with parole for his work on prison reform, Beckett would direct him in the role for the touring version of the San Quentin Drama Workshop in 1977. It was the only time he worked with a non-professional repertory company. Even if the untrained Cluchey lacked the intensity and range of some of the great actors who had tackled the role before him and after him, the production represented a culmination in Beckett's gradual refinement of the play over the course of eleven years directing the work. As a contemporaneous review put it:

> every detail is choreographed in a way so exact that the effort of holding it in place pulls the audience totally into the stage situation. At the same time, stylization is not allowed to dwindle into contrivance, a sense of urgency provides it with a rationale.
>
> (Mays 1982)

The balance between the realism of the spoken text and its physical stylization was central to Beckett's directorial approach to *Krapp's Last Tape*. His notebook illustrated a painstaking elaboration of each movement that structured the performance through repetition. No gesture stood in isolation: Krapp would move about his table in the same direction, would cock his head to listen, or turn the page of his ledger in a similar manner, even as Beckett reminded himself to "beware of excess stylization!" (Knowlson 1992, 81). Such tightly choreographed action exemplified Beckett's approach to the theatre as a medium that communicated visually and rhythmically, through stillness and movement, and the give and take of silence as much as whatever spoken word.

Some critics have argued that Beckett's plays reduce the actor to a puppet-like state; confined in the armature of the *mise-en-scène* and meticulous dictations about how long a pause should last, they are deprived of their independence. Such criticisms turn to the example of *Play*, with its three actors reduced to heads in urns facing front and issuing forth text, or *Not I*, where only a mouth remains, pinned to a beam of light and speaking on at breakneck speed. Actresses playing the latter part are often literally strapped into place to prevent any movement – employing apparatuses of sensory deprivation that resemble torture devices. Under the direction of Beckett, Krapp's comparative freedom of movement, his realistic wandering, is revealed as an illusory show. He, too, is straitjacketed by narrowly defined motions. For recurrences underline the habitual life of Krapp and illustrate how his rote way of living traps the man in his patterns.

And yet, it might be that we see the humanity of such a figure precisely in his struggle within and against the technology that confines him – a technology that includes not only the tape recording and the light overhead, but also, perhaps, the theatre itself, including of course the technology of acting. The profoundly individual nature of each performer is bared to our attention in the most restricted of quarters, the fact that, to recall Robbe-Grillet's comment on *Godot*, "he is there."

Most of these repetitions discovered while preparing to direct the later productions found their way into the revised script, though not all. For example, in his editorial comments on the notebook, Knowlson recounts a change unique to the 1970 production in France that was abandoned in the later German and English versions. In the moment when Krapp recalls sitting outside his mother's nursing home, "wishing she were gone" (221), the playwright changed the phrase to "burning for her to be gone," thus establishing a resonance with the older Krapp's later description of himself "shivering in the park, drowned in dreams and burning to be gone" (224). As Knowlson puts it, "through this small change of word, old Krapp is linked with his mother in a continuity of longing for suffering, her and his – in fact 'all that old misery' – to end" (Knowlson 1992, xviii). In his productions, Beckett decided to cut Krapp's singing ("Now the day is over,

/ night is drawing nigh-igh" [225]), feeling its premonition of an ending too overt, but found other ways to signal Krapp's preoccupation with death. As again described by Knowlson:

> in the 1969 Schiller-Theater production Krapp cast several anxious glances over his left shoulder, in case death itself should be waiting for him in the surrounding darkness. Beckett explained to Martin Held [who played Krapp in Berlin] "Old Nick's there. Death is standing behind him and unconsciously he's looking for it."
>
> (Knowlson and Pilling 1980, 82)

Never explicitly explained for its audiences, the repeated glance imbued the dark surrounds with added menace and established an underlying rhythm to the monologue.

Many of Beckett's later plays focus on a lone figure physically isolated on stage and often psychologically isolated in lasting memories: May in *Footfalls* (1976), the male figure in *Ghost Trio* (1977), the speaker in *A Piece of Monologue* (1979), the Woman in *Rockaby* (1980), and so on. The play that in many ways most resembles *Krapp's Last Tape*, however, is Beckett's *Happy Days* (1961). Here a middle-aged woman, Winnie, is fixed centerstage and buried to her waist in a mound of dried earth. She goes through the motions of her daily ablutions and preparations, passing the time and speaking incessantly as if nothing were the matter. In the second act of the play, she has been buried up to her neck and yet she continues onwards, repeating her rounds largely oblivious and outwardly optimistic about the weather. Her habits, like Krapp's, define her day and her self.

In the Belgian theatre company NT Gent's 2008 production of *Krapps laatste band* (directed by Johan Simons, with

Steven Van Watermeulen as Krapp), Krapp's table was perched atop a mound of dirt. Like an archeologist working at the layers of the past, he dug in the muck to unearth his bottle and belongings, as well as material remains from a more distant past: a woman's lace bodice, a pram wheel. Apart from brief lapses when she registers the horror of her resolute capture, Winnie persists in her customary living because it is the only thing she can do. Krapp had no such excuse, for he freely paws through the dust of time.

The composer Marcel Mihalovici suggested a more explicit adaptation of the play when he approached Beckett in 1961 about setting the French version of the text to music to create the opera *Krapp ou la dernière bande*. It was the first of Beckett's texts adapted into an operatic work (in 1977 he would write a sixteen-line poem as the text for the experimental composer Morton Feldman's only opera *Neither*) and the playwright, who listened avidly to classical music, was closely involved in the process of creation. Mihalovici recounts their working relationship: "Beckett on occasion caused me to make changes in what I showed him in the score, he either approved or disapproved, made me modify certain stresses in the vocal line, while at the same time helping me to look for others" (Calder 1967, 21). Sometimes described as "too lush and Romantic for Beckett," the composition nonetheless highlights the manner in which the play is a work for, and on, the voice (Knowlson 1996, 418).

In a more visual register, Robert Wilson's 2009 production of the play exaggerated the character's conflicted desire for disembodiment and divorce from romantic tendencies. An intensely imagistic director who, like Krapp, often stages conflicts between light and dark on a formal and abstracted plane, Wilson set Krapp's table in front of a gridwork of close vertical lines that suggested both the divided shelves of his archive and the bars of a prison. With their geometric precision, they became a measuring device against which his form might take shape and proportion. On either side of the desk long tables hemmed him in, each piled high with stacks of paper – his work another barrier to whatever outside world. In his first solo performance since playing Hamlet in 2000, Wilson himself portrayed Krapp in clownlike white pancake makeup, his signature sudden expressionistic gestures and poses distinguishing the embodied Krapp from the recorded in drastic sculptural figurations. Wilson premiered the work on the eve of his own sixty-ninth year, thus suggesting a connection between his biography and that of Beckett's alter ego. This intersection between performer and role seems inevitable in the case of Krapp.

Some of the greatest stage actors of the past fifty years have tackled *Krapp's Last Tape* and we are fortunate enough to have accessible recordings of many of these performances. The piece lends itself to the camera, with its attention on the face of the listener and its relatively stagnant stage image. Indeed, Beckett would expand on this facet of the play in his subsequent work for television, *Eh Joe* (written in 1965 – incidentally, the only other script he titled after a named character). Here, the camera begins by following the eponymous Joe around a small uniform room, as he systematically shuts off the outside world by closing curtain, door, and window. Having thus set the stage *à la* Krapp, the remainder of the piece consists almost entirely of the distant camera drawing closer and closer to the silent protagonist, watching his response head-on as he sits on his bed and faces out, listening to the voice of a woman from his past, who drowned herself because he abandoned her. In some twisted possible world, this might be the aftermath of Krapp's separation from the girl on the punt. Joe never says a word, but the several versions that have been filmed offer significantly different interpretations of his character and his relationship to the voice, all communicated by a furrow of the brow, a curve of the mouth, a sudden gasp of relief or sorrow. Krapp is equally open to individual interpretation. As Beckett wrote in a letter to Pat Magee upon the completion of the monologue: "Krapp's face as he listens is of course three quarters of [the play's] battle. I made no attempt to indicate its changes and unchangingness, feeling that these could safely be left to you" (Beckett 2014, 120). So much of the "battle" of individual productions revolves around the nature of the performer and his particular face, it is as if the text became a kind of support for a portrait. In these last few pages, I would like to briefly discuss three such filmed performances of *Krapp's Last Tape* that are widely available in digital format on the internet and in DVD and VHS recordings. While none of these performances makes the kind of marked interventions of Wilson or the NT Gent production mentioned above, their subtle choices are worthy of our attention.

Fourteen years after performing in the premiere production of the monologue that had been written for him, Magee once again took on the role of Krapp in a television version for the BBC. Donald McWhinnie, the director of the Royal Court premiere in 1958, helmed the production. Magee's garret is a large and terribly bare chamber of grey walls and slanting geometries of light, that second area where Krapp stores his boxes of tapes, machine, and booze an opening at the rear of the room. There is nothing on the walls, no furniture, apart from a simple table and chair with the requisite light hanging overhead. It feels uninhabited, as if Krapp has entered the room only for this occasion, but cannot live here. Contrary to the stage directions in the original script, where we discover Krapp already looking out over his machine and boxes, McWhinnie follows Beckett's revised script from 1969 and has the old man laboriously carry everything from the back and put it into place. Over a couple of trips, we watch the stage being set.

Magee's Krapp devours his bananas with a grotesque lasciviousness, tearing off the skins by the handful and caressing the flesh with a quasi-sexual fervor. He keeps stumbling into the back room in short, shuffling steps, using the wall to support his thick and unwieldy frame, casting a vast shadow that shrinks and looms with every journey back and forth. This Krapp is a mess, ungainly and sloppy in a loose, stained white shirt and dark vest. The camera pulls in and out with a mechanical directness, often in close-up on Krapp as he listens, cupping his ear in one hand. Sometimes it watches him in profile, sometimes from the front – a number of shifts of angle and focus. Magee's "present" voice is a squeaking whine, all nasal, while the younger tapebound self has a nearly unctuous resonance of long vowels and sonority.

It is an absolutely captivating performance, watching Magee listen as his eyes scan whatever distance, in a rapid back and forth as if he were reading some text or glancing from eye to eye of some invisible interlocutor. Like us, he seems to hear this for the first time, by turns horrified, devastated, and aroused by what he hears. His unshaven jaw hangs open and the measure of his breath guides our own pace of listening. When he hears the passage about the punt, he lowers his head to the table, his hand falling across the tape machine and drawing the camera's focus so that we can only see the bowed form at the rear of the shot. This close up we can see the sweat glistening on Krapp's brow, the visible mark of the strain of listening that gathers in occasional drops on his nose, down his cheek. Or are they tears that he blinks away?

Krapp's world began to expand outwards in Beckett's later productions, with their incorporation of that second lit area; more recent performances after Beckett's death in 1989 fill out the space in detail. Filmic conventions push this representation of reality to an extreme and it is in the adaptation of the play for the *Beckett on Film* project in 2001 that we find a nearly exhaustive realism. The film begins with rainstreaked shadows cast on Krapp through a window, from which direction the camera looks on. We hear the rain's monotonous downfall, wind, or thunder shuddering in the distance, and the sounds of this outside world continue under the scene until they are eventually subsumed into the crackles of the tape and dissipate. Shelves overflowing with boxes and papers are just visible in dimly lit corners of the room. The whole scene is dense with stuff.

In 2001, at the instigation of Michael Colgan, the artistic director of Dublin's Gate Theatre, new film versions of all nineteen of Beckett's plays were prepared, each directed, designed, and performed by a different team of theatre, film, and visual artists. Some of these productions took more liberties than others, and with varying degrees of success. The Canadian film director Atom Egoyan remediated a stage production of *Krapp's Last Tape* that Colgan himself had directed the year before for the Gate with the British actor John Hurt. The stage production has had its own recurring life since: it has been revived twice – in 2006 and again in 2011, when Hurt was 71 and looked even more like Beckett with his craggy brow, gaunt cheeks, and spiked hair.

In saying that the production was a "remediation," I mean that the content of one medium (theatre) was appropriated by another medium (film), so that the nature of both media might become apparent (see Bolter and Grusin 1998). Of course, this was the case with all the *Beckett on Film* pieces, but by virtue of the fact that *Krapp's Last Tape* filmed a stage production that had been prepared by a different director, it seemed particularly situated to address the divergent technologies of theatre and film. Egoyan says that reading Beckett's work greatly influenced his own work:

> this play in particular, *Krapp's Last Tape*, had a huge effect on me as a teenager. It changed my whole view about how people react to technology [. . .] Filming the play adds another layer. We are making a recording of a play about a man recording his life. I wanted to integrate all that into the language of the film. To do this, we used very long takes, during which you become aware of time, and not using a lot of cutting. [. . .] The camera doesn't just record the performance, it participates in it.
>
> (Egoyan n.d.)

In Egoyan's hands the camera is a relatively unobtrusive spectator. In slow but nearly constant motion it tracks in Krapp through long takes that last upwards of fourteen minutes. A sudden jerk pulls back when he fast-forwards through the jetty scene, as if Krapp were pushing away both modes of recording at the same time.

Hurt is vicious here, momentarily battering the tape machine and the table, then barking out his curse – in Hurt's interpretation the expectoration "balls!" – with frightening malice. Indeed, the older Krapp we see before us shifts quite abruptly throughout from bombast to a lyric softness, almost too much variation for the intimacy of the camera – perhaps indicating some trace of Hurt's stage performance? Hurt creaks with bitterness and bursts with violence. In the end of the piece, Hurt waves his hands over the machine as it rewinds that last time as if he could push along the spool, or conjure the event from the air through the pass of a hand – his sudden total stillness upon restarting the reel at the memory of the punt is shocking. As the tape plays out one final time, he sits staring forwards, eyes locked with the camera as it sidles closer and closer. The voice on the recording subsides, but we can still hear the reel turning, as unrelenting as time, and still the camera draws closer to Hurt's unmoving stare. A tear hangs in place in his left eye. We wait interminably, in close-up, until a sudden blackout.

Perhaps the most remarkable version of *Krapp's Last Tape* on record gathers its force in part because the performer and the character shadow one another so closely. In October 2006, while suffering from the esophageal cancer that would take his life two years later, the great British actor-playwright Harold Pinter took to the stage a last time to play *Krapp's Last Tape* for a brief ten-performance run directed by Ian Rickson at the Royal Court Theatre. The filmed version was captured by three cameras during a single performance after the run had concluded. There were no retakes or revisions.

Pinter had seen the original production of the play with Magee performing Krapp in 1958. Later, when directing the first revival of his own seminal play *The Birthday Party* with the Royal Shakespeare Company in 1964, he cast the actor in one of the roles. Beckett's influence on Pinter is well documented: in plays composed of language hollowed out by silence, in situations of abandonment and hopeless waiting, we might say he continued Beckett's project of mining impotence. Pinter's investigation, however, sought to expose the impotent individual to the impersonal and inscrutable menace of power. One of the greatest dramatists of the twentieth century, Pinter was far removed from the failures of Krapp – like Beckett, he received a Nobel Prize for his work – but like Beckett's fictional other, here was a writer looking back at his life from the furthest edge. As one reviewer explained the experience of watching the performance: "You often feel that you're suddenly seeing in three dimensions, as if two slides – a Beckett/Krapp and a Pinter – are being superimposed on each other" (Clapp 2006).

On a stage strewn with boxes and paper detritus, Pinter played the part from an electric wheelchair – a necessity because of his debilitated state, yet also a nod to *Endgame*'s wheelchair-bound protagonist, the storyteller Hamm – only rising to unsteady feet for the curtain call at the end. Any comic roughness had been pared away; the banana business was cut from the production, as was the anxious pacing. Instead, the bracing and brooding presence of Pinter himself filled the stage. One heard his sensitivity to the give and take of pause and silence, his pleasure in the sound of language, and the gruff and raspy grain of a voice passing through its cancerous threshold. Even on film there is a vertiginous materiality to the time of the performance, knowing that this evening is passing for performer and for character, that this will have been the last time he appears on a stage. An unseen but not unfelt death hovers in the dark, towards which Pinter/Krapp looks twice. We cannot see it, but it sits close to him. When he pulls the current tape from the machine in order to listen once more to the passage about the girl on the punt, he hurls it to the ground, presumably destroying it or unraveling it irreparably. No more, his body says, this game is over.

I have felt this peculiar exposure of the individual actor in Beckett's plays and films of his plays more viscerally than in any other playwright's work I have encountered. I think of John Gielgud's final performance as the Protagonist in the *Beckett on Film* version of Beckett's *Catastrophe* (directed by David Mamet in 2000). The playwright's penultimate work for the theatre shows a Director ordering his female Assistant to manipulate a lone actor onstage. They are rehearsing for a performance, constructing a kind of minimalist *tableau vivant* centered on the body of this precarious figure. The Protagonist is treated like an object, mounted on a plinth like some sculpture, exposed in an increasingly dehumanized manner to the demands of an authority whose dictates closely resemble those Beckett makes of his performers (recall *Not I*'s torturous machine). The figure is passive throughout until the final moment when, in the last glare of light after the rest of the space has gone dark, he raises his head and fixes the audience with his gaze. The script doesn't tell us what that stare says, only that its communication stops the audience in its tracks, and brings the performance to a halt. In the film, the camera skirts the shadowed form until this final moment where the light and frame reveal Gielgud himself centerstage. There stands that great actor most known for his mellifluous voice, silent then in this brief ten-minute performance and silent forever afterwards. By the time the film was released, Gielgud had died. And the actor who plays the Director in this filmed version of *Catastrophe*? Harold Pinter.

It is the look, again, that confirms the performer's singular presence. Gielgud's lasting gaze in that fugitive glimpse before he turns away forever; and here, too, "when the critics faced Pinter in *Krapp's Last Tape* they found themselves, above all, subjected in return to Pinter's unique gaze"

(Stokes 2009, 223). In his account of Pinter's final performances, John Stokes references two critics who saw in
Pinter's stare out either a look into the void or a look into
their very being: "the old-fashioned curtain fell away. There,
on an almost bare, twilit stage, and fixing me, a mere six
feet away, with a confident glare of his significant eyes, was
Mr Pinter himself" (De Jongh 2006).

And I suppose that this is the wonder of Beckett's play, at
least for me as I look back at it again and again over the years.
It is a glass through which to see another life isolated and
exposed: it shows Pinter himself in relief against the dark surround, it shows Magee melting under his lone lamp – gone
now, both gone. But it is also a glass in which one might
see oneself reflected, or a past or future version of the same.
And so I frequently return to the play in the manner that
Krapp returns to his tapes, wondering where I might be in
there. Perhaps the play acquires its fullest force through such
repetitive encounters, as we age and look forward towards
what could be, and back at what could have been. What is
missing, of course, in this pull to past and future, is the present itself: the capacity to live in the moment that the theatre
demands of us again and again, every night anew.

So where is Krapp now? Nearly 60 years old, the technology that shares the stage with that old man and acts alongside him is a thing of the past, yet *Krapp's Last Tape* feels as
relevant as ever. We live in a time of constant and thorough
self-documentation, our photographs and messages accumu-
lating in a bottomless archive of Facebook posts and Gmail
messages. Surrounded by his own yearly status updates, Krapp
appears an eerie premonition of this tendency to record
everything. He's given up trying to put a good face on the
situation, to pose as the great intellectual or artist so full of

potential, but what else is there for him to hold onto apart from this steady translation of the self into the recording? He can embrace his machine as if it were some substitute for the human contact that he has abandoned, even for the person he once was, but that evening in the future is a lonely one: a single figure and the technologies that anchor him to appearance – the book, the tape, the theatre. We are more fortunate, for we can leave the desk behind, walk out of the darkened room, out of the theatre. We can leave behind our habits, the same old words about what has been and what might be. We can be again, *without* the same old misery, even as Krapp remains, looping endlessly from present to past, from real to reel.

References

Barthes, Roland (1977). "The Grain of the Voice." In *Image-Music-Text*. Translated by Stephen Heath. New York: Farrar, Strauss, and Giroux. 179–189.

Beckett, Samuel (1983). *Disjecta: Miscellaneous Writings and a Dramatic Fragment*. London: John Calder.

Beckett, Samuel (1989). *Proust and Three Dialogues with Georges Duthuit*. London: John Calder.

Beckett, Samuel (2010a). *The Selected Works of Samuel Beckett, Vol. II: Novels*. New York: Grove Press.

Beckett, Samuel (2010b). *The Selected Works of Samuel Beckett, Vol. III: Dramatic Works*. New York: Grove Press.

Beckett, Samuel (2014). *The Letters of Samuel Beckett, Vol. III: 1957–1965*. Cambridge: Cambridge University Press.

Bergson, Henri (1911). *Laughter: An Essay on the Meaning of the Comic*. Translated by Cloudesley Brereton and Fred Rothwell. Mineola, NY: Dover Publications.

Bolter, Jay David and Richard Grusin (1998). *Remediation: Understanding New Media*. Cambridge, MA: MIT Press.

Borges, Jorge Luis (1999). *Collected Fictions*. Translated by Andrew Hurley. New York: Penguin.

Calder, John, ed. (1967). *Beckett at 60: A Festschrift*. London: Calder and Boyars.

Carlson, Marvin (2002). *The Haunted Stage: Theatre as a Memory Machine*. Ann Arbor, MI: University of Michigan Press.

Clapp, Susannah (2006). "Clarity in His Master's Voice." *Guardian.* October 22.

Cohn, Ruby (1962). *Samuel Beckett: The Comic Gamut.* New Brunswick: Rutgers University Press.

Cohn, Ruby (1980). *Just Play: Beckett's Theater.* Princeton: Princeton University Press.

Cohn, Ruby (2006). "A Krapp Chronology." *Modern Drama* 49, no. 4: 514–524.

Connor, Steven (2007). *Samuel Beckett: Repetition, Theory and Text.* Aurora: The Davies Group Publishers.

Connor, Steven (2014). *Beckett, Modernism and the Material Imagination.* Cambridge: Cambridge University Press.

De Jongh, Nicholas (2006). "Pinter's Last Look Back in Anger." *Evening Standard.* October 16.

Dukore, Bernard (1973). "*Krapp's Last Tape* as Tragicomedy." *Modern Drama* 15, no. 4: 531–534.

Egoyan, Atom (n.d.). "Egoyan on Beckett." *Beckett on Film.* Accessed September 20, 2015. www.beckettonfilm.com/plays/krappslasttape/interview_eg.html.

Fletcher, John and John Spurling (1972). *Samuel Beckett: A Study of His Plays.* New York: Hill and Wang.

Hesla, David H. (1971). *The Shape of Chaos: An Interpretation of the Art of Samuel Beckett.* Minneapolis, MN: University of Minnesota Press.

Kalb, Jonathan (1989). *Beckett in Performance.* Cambridge: Cambridge University Press.

Kenner, Hugh (1961). *Samuel Beckett: A Critical Study.* New York: Grove Press.

Knowlson, James (1976). "*Krapp's Last Tape*: The Evolution of a Play, 1958–1975." *Journal of Beckett Studies* 1 (1976): 50–65.

Knowlson, James, ed. (1980). *Samuel Beckett: "Krapp's Last Tape"; A Theatre Workbook.* London: Brutus Books.

Knowlson, James, ed. (1992). *The Theatrical Notebooks of Samuel Beckett: Krapp's Last Tape.* New York: Grove Press.

Knowlson, James (1996). *Damned to Fame: The Life of Samuel Beckett.* New York: Simon and Schuster.

Knowlson, James and James Pilling (1980). *Frescoes of the Skull: The Later Prose and Drama of Samuel Beckett.* New York: Grove Press.

Koestenbaum, Wayne (2001). *The Queen's Throat: Opera, Homosexuality, and the Mystery of Desire*. Boston, MA: Da Capo Press.

Lawley, Paul (2015). "Krapp at the Hawk's Well: Beckett, Yeats, and Joyce." *Modern Drama* 58, no. 3: 370–390.

Lyons, Charles R. (1983). *Samuel Beckett*. New York: Grove Press.

Mays, J. C. C. (1982). "The San Quentin Drama Workshop: *Krapp's Last Tape* and *Endgame*, directed by Samuel Beckett." *Journal of Beckett Studies* 8: 136–140.

Mercier, Vivan (1977). *Beckett/Beckett*. New York: Oxford University Press.

Ong, Walter (1982). *Orality and Literacy: The Technologizing of the Word*. London: Methuen.

Pronko, Leonard C. (1962). *Avant-Garde: The Experimental Theatre in France*. Berkeley, CA: University of California at Berkeley Press.

Robbe-Grillet, Alain (1965). *For a New Novel: Essays on Fiction*. Translated by Richard Howard. New York: Grove Press.

Scarry, Elaine (2001). *Dreaming by the Book*. Princeton, NJ: Princeton University Press.

Shenker, Israel (1956). "Moody Man of Letters." *New York Times*, May 6, sec. 2:3.

Stokes, John (2009). "Pinter's Last Tapes." In *The Cambridge Companion to Harold Pinter*, 2nd edn. Edited by Peter Raby. New York: Cambridge University Press. 216–230.

Tóibín, Colm (2006). "Pinter Takes on Beckett." *Telegraph*, October 7.

Index